ENVIRONMENTAL ISSUES

WATER AROUND THE WORLD

By Gemma McMullen

KidHaven
PUBLISHING

Published in 2017 by
KidHaven Publishing, an Imprint of Greenhaven Publishing, LLC
353 3rd Avenue
Suite 255
New York, NY 10010

© 2017 Booklife Publishing
This edition is published by arrangement with Booklife Publishing

Designer: Ian McMullen
Editor: Gemma McMullen

Cataloging-in-Publication Data

Names: McMullen, Gemma.
Title: Water around the world / Gemma McMullen.
Description: New York : KidHaven Publishing, 2017. | Series: Environmental issues | Includes index.
Identifiers: ISBN 9781534520530 (pbk.) | ISBN 9781534520554 (library bound) | ISBN 9781534520547 (6 pack) | ISBN 9781534520561 (ebook)
Subjects: LCSH: Water–Juvenile literature.
Classification: LCC GB662.3 M36 2017 | DDC 333.91–dc23

Printed in the United States of America

CPSIA compliance information: Batch #CW17KL: For further information contact Greenhaven Publishing LLC, New York, New York at 1-844-317-7404.

Please visit our website, www.greenhavenpublishing.com. For a free color catalog of all our high-quality books, call toll free 1-844-317-7404 or fax 1-844-317-7405.

Words in **bold** can be found in the glossary on page 24.

Photo Credits: Abbreviations: l–left, r–right, b–bottom, t–top, c–center, m–middle.
All images are courtesy of Shutterstock.com.

Coverb – Sergey Peterman. Coverlm - alexkar08. 2 - stocknadia. 3 - Valentyn Volkov. 4 - PopTika. 5 - Riccardo Mayer. 6 - Creative Travel Projects. 7t - Sergey Nivens. 7b - Dmitry Naumov. 10 - Mark Herreid. 11t - C_Eng-Wong Photography. 11b - Christophe Testi. 12l - limpido. 12mr - Valentyn Volkov. 13 - focal point. 14 - karelnoppe. 15tl - Diego Cervo. 15m- Tatyana Vyc. 16 - Halfpoint. 17tl- MANDY GODBEHEAR. 17tr - Sutichak. 17br - Keith Publicover. 18m - focusemotions. 18tl - A. and I. Kruk. 19b - Ami Parikh. 19l - Mark William Penny. 20b - Anticiclo. 20tr - HoleInTheBox. 21 - deamles for sale. 22b - Chirtsova Natalia. 22tr - Petr Malyshev. 23t - I love photo. 23b - Tomsickova Tatyana.

CONTENTS

WATER IS EVERYWHERE!

Water is everywhere! It covers three-quarters of our planet. From space, Earth looks blue because it is covered in so much water.

EARTH

Water is also inside us. Up to two-thirds of the human body is made up of water. We could not live without water. In fact, all living things need water to live.

WHERE DOES WATER COME FROM?

The water on Earth moves around in a water cycle. Water falls from clouds onto the ground.

THE WATER ON TOP OF MOUNTAINS STARTS TO ROLL DOWN THE MOUNTAINSIDES IN STREAMS, WHICH JOIN WITH LAKES, THEN RIVERS, AND, EVENTUALLY, OCEANS.

WHEN WATER IN THE OCEANS IS HEATED BY THE SUN, IT RISES UP INTO THE SKY AND FORMS CLOUDS.

WHEN IT GETS COLD ENOUGH, THE WATER FALLS, AND THE CYCLE STARTS AGAIN.

THE WATER CYCLE

The water rises when it is heated by the sun. This is called **EVAPORATION.**

The water flows to the ocean through streams and rivers. This is called **COLLECTION.**

OCEAN

The water makes clouds, which are blown by the wind. This is called **CONDENSATION.**

Water falls on a mountain. This is called **PRECIPITATION.**

RAIN

SNOW

MOUNTAIN

STREAM

RIVER & LAKE

9

CLOUDS

Clouds are made up of water. Clouds send rain, sleet, and snow down to Earth. There are many different types of clouds. Some of the main ones are:

CUMULUS CLOUDS

CUMULUS CLOUDS ARE LARGE AND PUFFY. CUMULUS CLOUDS CAN TYPICALLY BE SEEN IN GOOD WEATHER. THEY ARE CLOSE TO THE GROUND.

CIRRUS CLOUDS

CIRRUS CLOUDS ARE THIN AND WISPY. THEY ARE OFTEN WHITE OR GRAY IN COLOR. CIRRUS CLOUDS ARE ACTUALLY MADE OF ICE.

STRATUS CLOUDS

STRATUS CLOUDS LOOK LIKE LAYERS OF FLAT CLOUDS. THEY OFTEN SIGNAL THAT RAIN IS ON ITS WAY.

FORMS OF WATER

Water comes in three forms.

LIQUID

The water that we drink is liquid. Liquid moves around easily and changes shape to match its container.

ICE

When water is frozen, it turns into ice. Ice is a solid. We use ice to cool down our drinks in the summer. The **polar regions** of Earth are covered with ice.

STEAM

WHEN WE HEAT WATER, IT TURNS INTO STEAM. STEAM IS A GAS. WE CAN SEE STEAM LEAVING A KETTLE ONCE THE WATER HAS BOILED.

Water can change its form repeatedly. Frozen water can be heated to make liquid, and steam can be cooled to make liquid, too.

HOW WE USE WATER

We use water in many different ways. Most importantly, we drink it. Every type of drink that you have is made of water!

Drinking enough water helps you stay healthy!

We also use water for washing ourselves and our clothes, for cooking, for cleaning, and even for flushing the toilet.

SAVING WATER

The water that comes into our homes is specially **treated** before we use it to ensure that it is clean and safe to use. It is important that we do not waste water. This is because Earth's **population** is growing, and we need to make sure there is enough water for everyone to use.

Millions of people live without access to clean and safe water.

There are some simple things we can do to save water. We can take showers rather than baths, since showers use much less water than baths do. We can turn the faucet off while we brush our teeth, and we can use buckets of water to clean the car, rather than a hose.

It is important that we only use the water we need. When your parents make a cup of tea, ask them to only fill the kettle with the water they need.

WATER CAN BE WASTED THROUGH LEAKING TAPS, SO MAKING SURE OUR TAPS ARE WORKING CORRECTLY CAN HELP SAVE WATER.

RECYCLING WATER

We can recycle a lot of the wastewater we produce. The water used for cleaning vegetables or washing our hands can be reused to water plants in the garden. We can also collect rainwater to use in the same way. This means we don't need to use a hose to water the garden in the summer.

Did you know that used water is called gray water?

POLLUTION

When the air is heavily polluted, the pollution can get into the rain that falls back down to Earth. Polluted rain is called acid rain. Acid rain is dangerous for plants and animals and can cause them to die.

When water gets badly polluted, it cannot be treated for use. Therefore, it is important that we prevent water pollution to help our planet and protect the supply of drinkable water.

WATER FACTS

The five oceans on Earth are the Pacific Ocean, the Atlantic Ocean, the Arctic Ocean, the Southern Ocean, and the Indian Ocean.

Clean water has no smell and no taste.

Water is also used for fun. Water sports are a very popular **recreational** activity and include swimming, surfing, and water-skiing.

Ice and snow are used for ice-skating, ice hockey, skiing, and snowboarding.

23

GLOSSARY

polar regions areas in the Arctic and Antarctic, or near the North and South Poles

population the number of people that live in a place

recreational describing something done for enjoyment

treated cleaned using chemicals

INDEX